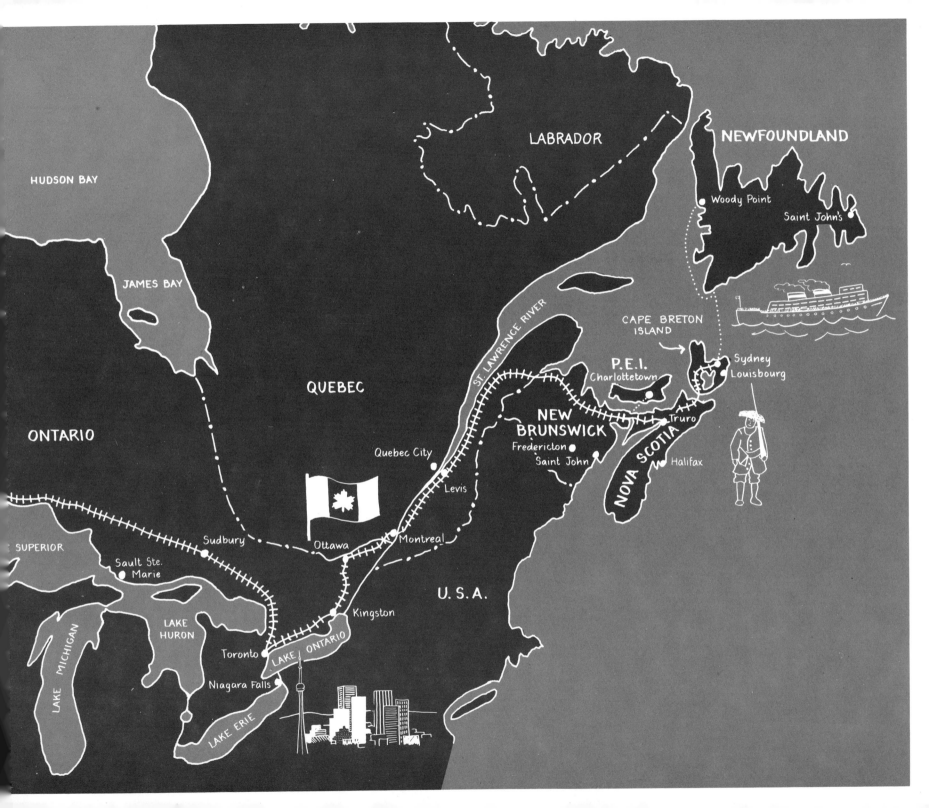

HUDSON BAY

JAMES BAY

LABRADOR

NEWFOUNDLAND

Woody Point

Saint John's

ONTARIO

QUEBEC

ST. LAWRENCE RIVER

CAPE BRETON
ISLAND

P.E.I.
Charlottetown

Sydney
Louisbourg

NEW
BRUNSWICK

Quebec City

Fredericton

Saint John

Truro

NOVA SCOTIA

Halifax

Levis

Sudbury

Ottawa

Montreal

SUPERIOR

U.S.A.

Sault Ste.
Marie

LAKE MICHIGAN

LAKE
HURON

Kingston

Toronto

LAKE ONTARIO

Niagara Falls

LAKE ERIE

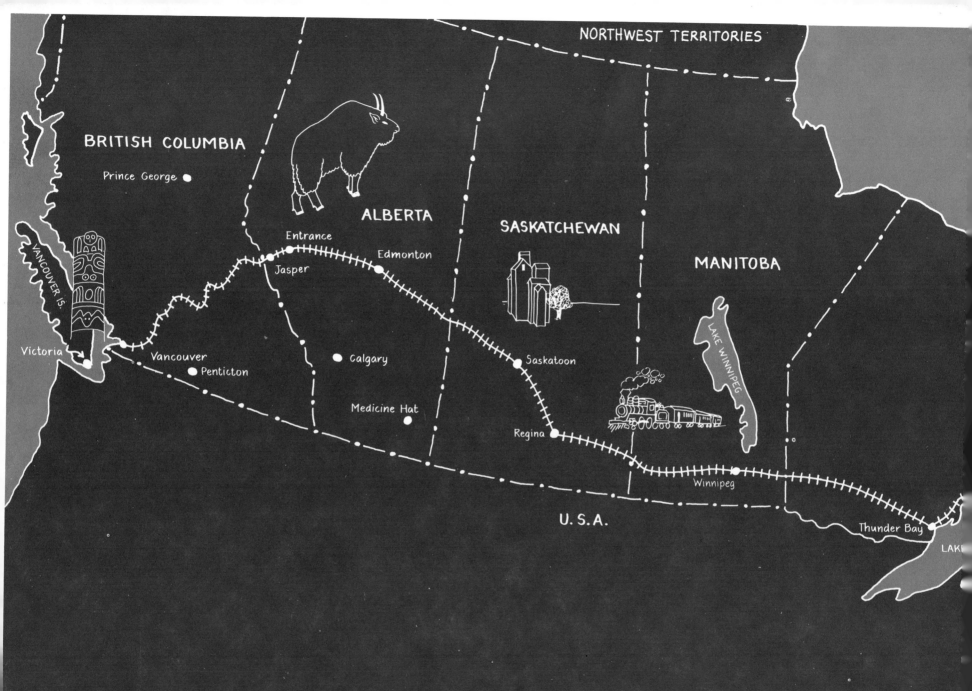

I t's a long way from Woody Point, Newfoundland, to Vancouver, British Columbia. It's a nine-and-a-half-hour plane trip and I usually sleep through most of it. I've slept my way across the country every year since I was four. But last summer was different. Last summer I took the train. All the way across Canada, coast to coast in fourteen days, all by myself. It was the biggest adventure of my life so far.

1

First, I'd better explain one or two things so that whole story makes sense. Woody Point is a small village on Bonne Bay on the west coast of Newfoundland. Gram lives there. Dad lives in Vancouver. I live both places. Last year, for instance, when Dad had to be away from home doing a lot of travelling, I spent the winter in Woody Point and went to school there. Now it's fall and I'm back with Dad, back at my old school in Vancouver. I guess it's sort of a complicated family arrangement. On the other hand, it makes life interesting, and it is the reason I was able to take my trip last summer.

I remember how I first got the idea, more than a year ago now. It was a hot, sunny morning, and it must have been low tide because my favourite rock was out of the water. I was sitting on it dangling my feet in the bay and thinking about Dad leaving for Vancouver the next day. All of a sudden a small, flat stone skimmed across the surface of the water. I whipped around and there he was, standing right behind me.

"I guess I don't need to start missing you yet," I said.

"Premature," he agreed. "You've got a letter."

It was from my cousin Julie in Saskatchewan. Dad sat down and waited for me to tell him the news. Julie is our most regular contact with my mother's family, so naturally he's always interested in what she has to say. I can hardly remember my mother at all. She died when I was just a little kid, but Julie still lives on a real ranch with ponies, not far from where my mother grew up. Julie and I are the same age and we'd written dozens, maybe hundreds, of letters to each other in the last two years. We'd become good friends that way, and I'd always wanted to visit her.

"Do you realize that you'll be flying right over Julie's farm tomorrow?" I asked Dad.

"Probably." He skipped another stone out to sea.

"Do you realize that we know people in almost every province and you'll actually fly over their houses and they won't even know it?"

He laughed and asked if I realized how much he had to do before he left. Then he disappeared up the hill to Gram's house.

It was at this point that I had my great idea. I saved it up to tell them at dinner because I wasn't sure what they'd think of it.

We had an enormous seafood feast that night to send Dad off. I waited until all three of us were well into the lobster. Then I said,

"When I go back to Vancouver I want to take the train."

"Why?" Dad asked. "Planes are faster."

"Because I want to visit Julie on her ranch."

"It's not a ranch. It's a pig farm." Dad didn't seem very excited about my idea.

"Well, whatever it is they have horses there, and I also want to stop in other places and really see Canada instead of just flying over it." Gram nodded but Dad said, "We'll see." When he says, "We'll see," in that particular tone of voice it means "Drop the subject."

After dinner some of the neighbours stopped in to say goodbye to Dad and it turned into a party. When I finally went to bed I was too excited to fall asleep right away. Gram and Dad were talking in the living room and snatches of their conversation kept drifting under my door.

"What do you think about this train notion, Stuart?"

"She's too young. It's a long way for a kid to travel alone."

There was a short silence, then Gram cleared her throat the way she does when she's about to say something serious.

"She'll be ten in June. I took to the Atlantic in my dory at that age. I don't see why Kate couldn't make it across the country in a train." It sounded as if Gram was on my side. I listened harder.

"I think it would be a marvellous experience for her, and it really wouldn't be more expensive than air fare."

"Well, it's not for a year. She'll probably forget about it."

"I doubt it. Anyway, I can't bear overprotected children."

I agreed with Gram. Of course I wasn't going to forget about it and I shouldn't be overprotected and it would be a marvellous experience and not much more expensive than the boring plane.

After Dad left the next day I really tried, but I'm not very good at pretending to be happy. Gram had been typing all afternoon and I'd been trying not to bother her. Finally she clicked off her machine and came over to give me a hug. "Nothing is a bigger waste of time than moping about things you can't change."

5

    I can hardly believe I was such a baby back then, but all I could say was, "I know," before I started sobbing. I wasn't going to see my own father for almost a year. Gram let me cry for a while longer and then she sent me down to the fish plant for some bait. We were going out jigging to catch some fresh cod for supper. When I met her at the dock she looked at me very seriously and asked if I'd managed to cheer myself up. I said I had. "Good. I've never allowed moping in the bow of my dory. Heave!"

    "Ho!" I answered and we were in the water.

    We rowed out into the bay and dropped the jigs over the side. It made me feel better just to look at Gram. She had such a peaceful expression on her face. Gram got her first dory when she was my age and she says that little boat set the pattern for her life. Even though she's lived in lots of places, she's happiest when she's sitting in her rubber boots in her dory in the sea. She doesn't fish for a living like lots of people in Woody Point. She works as a writer, but she says that writing is only her occupation. Fishing is her vocation.

I had a good year in Woody Point with Gram. I liked my school and I made a lot of new friends, and I certainly learned all about fishing. Once in a while I would mention my idea, my train trip to Vancouver. Gram always said, "We'll see," and went back to whatever she was doing.

We heard from Dad every couple of weeks. Sometimes he wrote long letters but more often he just sent postcards from towns in B.C. and Alberta. When he phoned at Christmas, Gram and I held the receiver between us so that we could all talk at once.

A family of whales arrived in early May and stayed in our bay for more than a month. They were still there on my birthday, which is June seventeenth. It happened to be a Saturday–a dismal, rainy one. I woke up early and went out to the kitchen to see what was up.

Gram was sitting at the table with a cup of coffee in front of her and her nose in a book, her usual morning pose. "Shhh!" she said, pointing to the big picture window. "The whales are celebrating something or other."

It was one of Gram's peculiarities that even though her house is on a hill across the road from the shore, she insisted on whispering whenever we watched the whales. I had tried to explain that we couldn't possibly disturb them from way up on the hill inside the house, but Gram always said, "Ssshh," and handed me the binoculars. I looked out of the window. There were three of them, diving and spouting and leaping right out of the water.

When I turned back to Gram she was reading again. I had a horrible thought: Was it possible that she had forgotten all about my birthday? "Nasty weather for the seventeenth of June," I said. Gram looked up, glanced at the whales and whispered, "Happy birthday, Kate."

I made my usual toast and eggs. Gram isn't much of a cook and she ignores breakfast altogether, except for insisting that I have some. When I came back to the table the whales had disappeared, Gram was talking normally and there was a fat, brown envelope beside my plate. I ripped it open and a huge pile of papers tumbled out onto the table. I thought I knew what it was all about, but I was too excited to believe it. I started to sort through the jumble. There was a sheaf of tickets that said "Via Rail Canada" with information about times and places in tiny computer writing. It was all right there in that envelope: my trip across Canada.

9

© Allinson and O'Kelly,
1979

An OWL Book
Published by Greey de
Pencier Books,
59 Front Street East,
Toronto
Printed in Canada
ISBN 0-919-872-43-3
hardcover
ISBN 0-919-872-44-1
paper

aboard!"

A cross-Canada adventure

Written and photographed
by Barbara O'Kelly
and Beverley Allinson

An OWL Book
Published by Greey de Pencier Books
Toronto, 1979

For the next few minutes I whooped and screamed and jumped around the room. I was going across Canada. I was going to visit Louisbourg and Montreal and Jasper and Julie in Saskatchewan. I couldn't sit still with fried eggs and toast. I charged over to give Gram a hug and spilled her coffee all over her book. She just laughed and said I was crazy like the whales.

Finally I calmed down enough to keep both my feet on the floor at once.

"Thank you, Gram."

"Not only me. Your father had something to do with it."

I rushed to the phone. "Can I call him?"

"Hold your horses. It's about four in the morning out there. He's calling you at suppertime."

We spent most of the day going through the package in a systematic sort of way. Gram explained about tickets and schedules and sleeping compartments, which are called roomettes, and when and where I'd stop and who would meet me. She had typed all the details on a sheet of paper that I was supposed to keep with my pocket money and never lose. Then we got out a huge map of Canada and traced the route from coast to coast.

We had fresh cod and birthday cake for dinner and Dad called just as I blew out the candles. Afterwards, Gram and I sat up late and talked. She is a far more experienced traveller than I was at the time and she loves to tell stories. I heard about the time her train was stuck in a tunnel in France all night long and how she lost her luggage in New York for almost a week. She'd travelled across Newfoundland by train, too, when the Newfie Bullet was running. In those days they had an actual employee called a wind sniffer who was hired to go out and sniff the wind and radio back with the weather report. They always took his word. If he said, "Blizzard," the Bullet didn't run that day.

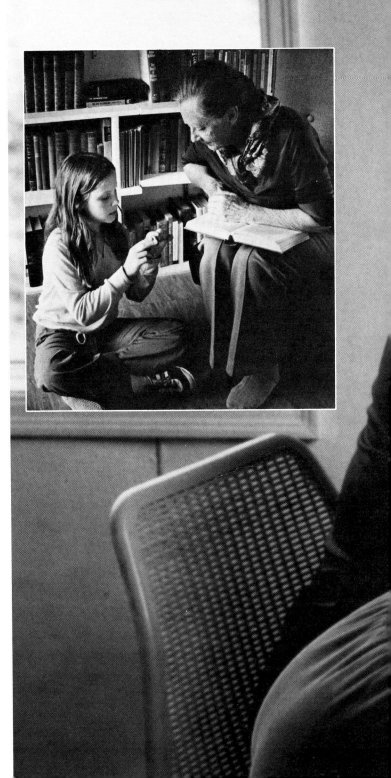

Gram and I had three more days together. At first we were very busy packing and remembering not to lose the schedule or the money or the tickets. I think Gram temporarily forgot how much she hates overprotected children. When I woke up on the morning of my last day in Woody Point I could smell the coffee and hear her typewriter clacking away.

We'd hurried to get everything done so we could spend the whole day together. I gulped down some breakfast while Gram finished what she was writing and we hit the main street just as the stores were opening.

Woody Point has three stores that sell everything at once–clothes, groceries, toys, hardware, rubber boots–well, everything. General stores, I guess they're called. The main street fronts right onto the sea and besides the general stores there are two restaurants, one gas station, a bar and a craft shop. There's also a fish canning plant where almost everyone's parents work unless they're actually out fishing.

We wandered up to Wilton's Café at one end of the village and back down to the fish plant to catch the ferry across to Norris Point. Then we hiked through the woods to the big hill where we always had our picnics. Norris Point is the highest place on Bonne Bay. You can see the villages of Woody Point and Birchy Head across the water and watch the matchbox ferry putting back and forth.

After lunch we went for a walk along our favourite beach and I found an abandoned lobster pot that was practically perfect. I decided to take it back with me and keep it in my bedroom to remind me of Woody Point. Gram laughed and said that real Newfoundlanders never keep lobster pots in their bedrooms, they use them to catch lobsters. She thought I was acting like a tourist, but I refused to leave it behind and she finally agree to send it to me.

15

The sun was setting in our eyes as we strolled home along the beach. I realized that it was over. The day had slipped by and there wouldn't be any more days like this for a long time. Tomorrow I'd be on the ferry on my way to the mainland. Tomorrow I'd have begun my trip and Gram would be back at her typewriter or out in her dory.

"You could come with me, Gram," I blurted, "and stay in Vancouver."

"No, I couldn't. And a long time ago you promised not to mope about things you can't change."

"I'll write you lots of letters."

"And I'll write back. We'll both be where we want to be. You'll be having a great adventure and I'll be having another summer in Newfoundland."

That was that. The next morning we packed the car and drove to Port aux Basques to catch the ferry. We talked about my trip all the way down. Gram had stopped telling me not to lose my tickets. I guess she'd just decided that I could take care of myself. We also didn't mention that we would miss each other.

The ferry was at the dock when we arrived. Gram gave me a last hug. "Go aboard now, Kate."

I picked up my bags and walked onto the ferry without even looking back at her. I wanted to go. I would not cry and I would not change my mind. I went up on the top deck and leaned over the railing. Gram was still standing there with her hands in her pockets and her collar turned up against the wind. All of a sudden she turned and strode off toward the parking lot. I watched until she was out of sight. She didn't look back either.

16

I left my bags at the information desk and set out to explore the Port aux Basques ferry. I went outside. The wind was whipping along the deck and big, grey clouds were rising right up out of the water. I'd heard lots of terrible stories about Atlantic storms from the fishermen around Woody Point but I was pretty sure that the Port aux Basques ferry never got lost at sea. All the same, I had to hold onto the rail and pull myself along against the wind to get back inside.

When I got to the lounge I noticed a kid about my age sitting by the window playing solitaire. I went over to watch and we made friends over a couple of games of gin rummy. His name was Michel and his family was moving to Fredericton, New Brunswick. All their furniture was in a moving van down on the car deck.

We had lunch together in the cafeteria–French fries with gravy and strawberry milkshakes–and it was delicious. Michel bought an extra carton of milk and we took it down to his station wagon where a big black cat and a little striped kitten were curled up on top of a box of blankets. They stretched and purred and ignored the milk. Michel said they liked to travel. The mother cat had already lived in Halifax, St. John's and Cornerbrook.

His mother found us later in the lounge and said we would be landing in North Sydney in less than an hour. I told her about my trip and she was amazed to hear that I was going all across Canada by myself. She also wanted to know who was going to meet me at the ferry dock. Richard was, I told her three or four times. She said I'd better stick with them until I found him and I said I would, just to make her feel better.

When the announcement came to return to the car decks, Michel and I rushed ahead and piled into the back seat with the cats. I got a little nervous about Richard because we had to wait until almost every other car was off. He would have expected me to come off first with the foot passengers.

Finally, it was our turn and we rolled up the ramp to Nova Scotia.

I spotted Richard immediately, leaning against the ramp, looking worried. "There he is!" I ran up to him with the whole family shouting after me: "Bye, Kate. Send a card. Enjoy your trip!"

Richard stopped frowning as soon as he saw me. He certainly looked different, all dressed up in a suit and tie. The last time I'd seen him, he'd been wearing jeans and a ratty old sweater–the kind that can't even remember what colour it used to be. I'd met him for the first time when he was camping near Woody Point. He came to visit Gram and told me all about his fort–the Fortress of Louisbourg. Well, it's not entirely his fort–it belongs to Parks Canada and he works there.

Richard is like Gram and Dad because they all have favourite subjects. Dad has music and books, and Gram has Newfoundland, fishing and books. With Richard, it's the fort. He knows everything there is to know about it and he tells it in a way that keeps you listening.

He talked about Louisbourg all the way there.

It was a French city and military post in the 1700s when Louis XIV and Louis XV were the kings of France. Number fourteen named it after himself, I guess. It was a big, important port back then, and this was before Canada existed, when France still owned Cape Breton. The fort was destroyed in 1760, and the new Louisbourg is what is called a reconstruction. It has been rebuilt so that every detail is exactly the same as it was in 1744.

The fort seemed a long way from Sydney. At last Richard slowed his car down at the top of a hill and pointed out the window. It was exactly the way Gram had described it, like driving into another century. Heavy grey clouds rose out of the ocean, and the grey stone walls of the fortress rose out of the mist.

We parked at the administration building and started across a drawbridge over a moat. "This is the Dauphin Gate," Richard

19

explained. "Those big lions are the symbols of the Bourbons, the French royal family. The crown prince was called the dauphin."

I knew all that. I'd read a book about the French revolution last winter. We were stopped in the middle of the drawbridge by a soldier with a musket and a bayonet. A big, serious sort of man came up behind him and stared us down. I glanced up at Richard. "Don't they know you work here?" "Sshhh," he said. "They're at war."

The second man began to boom at us. *"Vous entrez maintenant la forteresse et la ville de Louisbourg dans la colonie de l'Ile Royale."*

Richard translated in a quick whisper: "You are now entering the fortress and the city of Louisbourg in the colony of Isle Royale." The soldier glared at the interruption.

"Comme visiteurs étrangers pendant la présente guerre, vous devez laisser vos armes à feu ici avec le garde."

"As foreign visitors during the present war, you must leave your firearms here with the sentry," whispered Richard.

There was a lot more about curfews and breaking rules. Then the sentry clicked his heels together, snapped to attention and shouted: *"Vive le Roi!"*

Richard agreed that the king should have a long life and the soldier was ordered to let us pass: *"Soldat, laissez les passer."* We walked into Louisbourg. "Does he always do that?" I asked.

"That's his job," Richard told me. "He has to be careful. After all, we could be English spies."

I glanced back at the gate. The fierce-looking man stood with his arms folded, staring after us. "Who is he?" I whispered.

"Sergeant Jean Riviére."

That wasn't what I meant. I tried again. "But who is he *really*?"

Richard said, "He's really Sergeant Jean Riviére and this is really Louisbourg in the colony of Isle Royale. It's 1744 and France is at war with England."

I was beginning to understand.

The best thing about the fort is this: the people are still there just as they were more than 200 years ago. They live in the same houses, eat the same food, dress in the same clothes and work at the same jobs. The French soldiers are still in the barracks and the guard changes just as if the British fleet might sail into the harbour and attack at any minute.

It was late in the day and there weren't many people from either century as we walked up the Rue Toulouse. We visited the jail and the armory and passed two taverns on the main street. Auberge de l'Epée Royalle—the King's Arms—was where the officers and wealthy merchants spent their evenings. Just up the street, laughter floated through the door of a smaller, shabbier tavern. Richard said the soldiers spent their free time and most of their money there.

Richard had work to do and he asked if I'd mind exploring by myself for a while. I decided to go up on the battlements. I looked over the plains behind the fort and across the harbour in front of it, just the way the sentries used to. I leaned against a cannon and looked down at the Dauphin Gate as the last group of visitors headed for their tour bus and Sergeant Riviére raised the drawbridge.

I stared through the gloom at the rolling hills and imagined whole companies of British soldiers in their red coats, lurking in the trees, waiting for nightfall and the command to attack the fort. I shivered as the wind ripped along the battlements and right through my jacket. I imagined I heard the English drums far away in the hills.

I huddled in a sentry box, hugging myself to keep warm, trying not to think about ghosts. It had occurred to me that if a ghost wanted to haunt something and suddenly his home town came back, exactly as it was, well, naturally, that's what he would haunt.

It took some effort to leave my hiding place, and when I did I ran

all the way to the guard house where I was supposed to meet Richard. I sat down and hummed a song that I'd heard on the radio a lot. When I looked up, "it" was strolling toward me through the arch from the Governor's courtyard. At least it wasn't transparent or anything. It was wearing a plumed hat and powdered wig, breeches, stockings and funny pointed shoes. There was a sword swinging against its leg, but it didn't look like any of the soldiers I'd seen. It came closer. I held my breath. Of course it wasn't a ghost, it was only someone playing the part of a gentleman of 1744, someone who didn't know when to quit. Whoever it was came right up to me and bowed. He swept off his hat and said: "*Bonjour*. Good day. I am Monsieur de la Perelle, the town major."

"Hello," I answered.

"*Enchantée*. Are you enjoying your stay at Louisbourg?"

"Yes, thank you."

He continued on down the walk, stopping occasionally to gaze up

at the sky where the sun would have been setting, if there had been any sun. I watched him closely. Then it dawned on me. It was Richard! I went running up to catch him.

All night long I dreamed about the soldiers at Louisbourg. I kept going up to them and trying to explain that their war had been over for two hundred years, that this was Canada now, that they didn't have to guard the fort any more. But they couldn't see me or hear me and finally I ended up yelling at them: "You're all ghosts! You're stuck in the wrong century."

I woke up in a small, sunny room with flowers on the wallpaper. After a minute I remembered that I was at Richard's and that my trip had started yesterday. I jumped out of bed, threw on some clothes and ran downstairs.

Ten past nine–there was plenty of time. Richard called out from the kitchen. "You slept in. How do you feel about pancakes for breakfast?"

We ate a huge amount of food and set off for the station. We arrived half an hour early but I decided to get on the train anyway. We found my seat and Richard started worrying about me. I opened my knapsack and explained Gram's system: the tickets in the same order as the schedule, meal vouchers for the train and phone numbers for half the population of Canada, in case I got into trouble anywhere at all.

When he saw how organized I was, Richard remembered that he was late for the fort. As he rushed off I realized I hadn't thanked him. I scribbled a note and rapped on the window just as he was walking past. He looked up to wave and I held up my sign: "Thanks for Louisbourg and pancakes and everything."

27

I was sitting in one corner of a half-empty car. A Dayniter car it was called. That means that the seats tip back like a dentist's chair and almost turn into beds. I made myself comfortable and looked out the window. The station was moving. No–the train was moving. We were on our way! We crawled through Sydney, but as soon as we were out in the country, the train began to pick up speed. I leaned back and watched the tops of telephone poles flying by the clouds. It made me sleepy, so I jumped up and began exploring the train.

I walked through two more coaches exactly like mine, then the café-lounge, which is like a bar, and a dining room where waiters were getting ready to serve lunch. Past the kitchen there were three more coaches with seats that did not turn into beds. That section was crowded, probably because most people there would be getting off before it was time to go to sleep.

Trains have lots of washrooms and water fountains. They also have doors between cars that are the heaviest doors in the world. You have to brace yourself and pull with two hands to get them open and then you have to be fast or they'll shut on your foot. The platform between the doors is almost like being outside. You stand on a sheet of metal just over the place where the two cars are joined and it's very noisy but it's the best place on the train to feel the wheels clattering along the track.

I got back to my seat and started my journal. Gram had been very serious about this journal. She said that she expected facts when this trip was over. I'd just gotten to the French fries and gravy on the ferry with Michel when the conductor came to collect my ticket.

I looked out the window. We were passing through farm country, with cows and barns and little white houses. Now and again the train would stop at a town with a dark red railroad station. I wrote that down too.

At the second call for lunch I made my way to the café car. Joanne brought the menu and a glass of water. She was a student and this was the second summer she had worked as a waitress on the train. She said she made lots of money but it was hot work. The food was great and I was glad: I'd be eating a lot of it in the next two weeks.

I had to get off and on again at Truro with all my luggage, because this was where they added the sleeping cars and I was moving into my own compartment: car eleven-forty-one, roomette six. Harold was my sleeping-car attendant. He was very friendly and showed me how the seat in my little compartment turned into a bed. There was a big metal handle on the wall and when Harold pulled it the seat disappeared and a bed folded down: a real bed, with a mattress and sheets and pillows and blankets and everything.

I moved in and taped my pictures up on the wall. I thought it would be more like home if I could look up at Dad and Gram and Julie riding her pony Star. I put my toothbrush in the holder, tested the hot water and finished yesterday in my journal before the first call for dinner.

When I came back from the dining car, a little kid was leaning against the door of my roomette.

"My name is Megan. I saw you before so I came to visit. Do you want some of my sandwich?"

I didn't, but I invited her in anyway and she settled down with her sandwich and started chatting.

"What's your name? Oh? I don't know anybody else called Kate. I'm with my brother but he's just reading a book. He's fourteen and his name is Charles. I came to visit you because he's tired of talking to me."

I understood how he felt. She was a talkative little kid. "Where are you going?" I asked.

"Home. We get off at Amherst and take the bus to the ferry and the ferry to near Charlottetown and then my mom picks us up and drives us home. We've done it lots of times before."

"So you live on Prince Edward Island? Is the earth really red there?"

"Yeah. Everybody asks that. It's kind of brownish-red. I know why–because it has iron in it. I live on the Ark by the sea and I go to school in Dundas. I'm in Grade Two so I can read and everything and this summer I'm working. I pull weeds in the garden and I get a dime."

"Wait a minute," I interrupted her. "You just said that you lived on the *Ark*?"

"Yes."

"And your dad's name is Noah, right? And you have two of every kind of animal and you sail around looking for land?"

"Don't be crazy. We have two cats and my mother's name is Judy and we never sail anywhere except on the ferry to Amherst. We grow fish though."

"You *grow* fish?"

"Yeah. We grow lots of things and people come from all over on Sundays to see how we do it."

I repeated what she'd just said. "People come from all over on Sundays to watch you grow fish. Do you expect me to believe that?"

"It's true. The Ark is a famous place. Sometimes they write about it in magazines and once my picture was in one of them."

We heard a faint voice from the end of the corridor, calling, "Megan!"

"That's my brother. You can ask him if you don't believe me."

Her brother arrived, frowning. "Why do you always disappear like that? We have to get off soon."

"I went to find Kate. Tell her about the Ark, Charles."

Charles sat down, sighed and glanced at his watch. Then he glanced up at me. "Okay," he said. "The Ark is an experimental centre. We use solar energy and produce our own food by aquaculture as well as vegetable production, and...um...we recycle wastes and that kind of thing."

30

It sounded like a rehearsed speech. I wondered if anyone in this family spoke plain English.

Megan chimed in. "He means we live on a big farm and it's all heated by the sun and we grow fish and flowers and vegetables even in the winter in the greenhouse. Show her the picture, Charles."

Charles pulled out a photograph. "That's the Ark," he said.

I thought it was a pretty strange sort of house and I said so. Charles smiled for the first time. "It's not a house exactly." He pointed to most of the glass wall in the photo. "The front part is a greenhouse and those black panels on the top are solar collectors. They capture the sun's heat. That's how we get hot water. And that's how the house is heated in the winter."

Megan tugged impatiently at his sleeve. "Now, tell her about the fish," she ordered.

"Then there are the experiments in aquaculture," Charles said.

"Aquaculture," I repeated. "You mean growing things in water?" Charles nodded and I glanced at Megan. "So you do grow fish?"

"That's one of my jobs," said Charles. "We breed a kind of tropical fish that tastes a lot like trout. We hatch the eggs, the fish grow and then we eat some of them and breed more from the others. I have to clean the tanks—we use the water for the plants."

"Yeah, I know about recycling. My grandmother has a compost heap. What else do you do?"

Charles scratched his head. "Well, I'm in charge of the mowing—there's a lot of grass to cut every week. I drive the tractor sometimes and I'm helping to build the barn."

"I weed the garden," Megan added. "I get paid a dime and I'm learning to swim. We're right beside the ocean."

I laughed. "It sounds like a great place to live."

There was a knock at the door and the call: "Five minutes to Amherst." Charles stood up. "That's us. Nice meeting you." Megan jumped up and repeated: "Nice meeting you."

33

As soon as they left, I pulled my bed down, crawled in and sat propped up on the pillows watching the New Brunswick night fly by the window. I opened my journal and wrote "Day Two" at the top of a fresh page. I wanted to write down everything about the Ark and solar energy and aquaculture before I forgot it. Then I turned out the light and listened to the wheels humming along the rails and the groan as the train shifted around the bends. I thought about all the other passengers, sleeping foot to head to foot in their separate boxes as the train raced along the track. It reminded me of the conveyor belt at the fish plant in Woody Point.

The next thing I knew, it was daylight. I checked my watch and it said nine, but I knew it was only eight because we'd changed from Atlantic to Eastern time somewhere in New Brunswick in the middle of the night. It was a nasty, drizzly day. The track was running along beside a river. The St. Lawrence? Yes, we were in Quebec.

There was a knock on the door and it was Harold about breakfast. By the time I arrived at the dining car, everybody else had left so I got to eat at the special staff table with Harold and the other conductors. We made a long stop at Levis in the middle of breakfast. We looked across the river at Quebec City and I thought it was the most beautiful place I'd ever seen. The ships anchored in the harbour looked like toys, and the city itself wound around the side of a big hill with a castle at the top. Harold laughed and said it was only the Château Frontenac, and it wasn't a castle at all, just a big hotel.

"But doesn't *château* mean castle?" I asked. "Frontenac Castle?"

Back in my roomette the bed had turned back into a seat. I sat down and wondered what to do with myself. We were passing through more farm country. Now and again we'd stop at little towns–the same red stations, white church steeples and rain. Mostly it looked very wet out. The names were all in French and the licence plates on the cars said: *"Québec: Je me souviens."*

I spent the morning wandering around the train. I talked to a few people: a little kid, even younger than Megan, an old miner from Cape Breton on his way to visit his son in Montreal and two school teachers from Halifax. Gradually the scenery began to change. There were fewer farms and more factories and shopping plazas. We'd lost the St. Lawrence again and a big expressway ran along beside the track. I decided this was the beginning of Montreal.

I hadn't been in a big city for almost a year. I didn't really know anybody in Montreal–I would be staying with Luc and Jeannine but I hardly knew them at all. I began to worry about French. I stood in front of the mirror and practised: *"Bonjour, je m'appelle Kate."*

Harold stopped in and asked if I was all packed. I leaned out of the bathroom and answered, *"Oui."*

We pulled into a huge underground station. Place Ville Marie-Gare Centrale. Central Station. I knew that. It was the biggest station I'd ever seen. It would be easy to lose your friends here.

I went straight to the green light at the information booth. That was supposed to be our meeting place, but I couldn't see Luc anywhere. I sat down on my suitcase. Maybe he had the days mixed up. Maybe he'd forgotten. Maybe he was here and I didn't recognize him. I tried to remember what he looked like. I knew he was tall. I was checking out a tall man in a trench coat who didn't look familiar when another tall man with a little kid on his shoulders came up and said: "Hi, Kate. Hope you haven't been waiting long." Of course! *That's* what he looked like.

Luc introduced me to Justine who was two and a half years old and only spoke French. She kept asking me questions that I couldn't understand. I explained to Luc that I didn't really speak French very well yet. He laughed. "Don't worry. Neither does she. Come on, I'll give you a fast tour of beautiful Montreal in the rain and then we'll go shopping."

We found the car in the underground lot. Justine continued to babble. "What is she asking me?"

"Well, she wants to know if you like big blue trucks, if you know her *maman* and whether you think horses smell bad."

I thought for a minute and answered her: *"J'aime les camions bleus."*

We drove to the top of Mont Royal, right in the middle of the city. Luc said it was efficient sightseeing—the whole city at once. Justine bounced around in the front seat and crawled all over me. She must have spotted twenty blue trucks and they all struck her as wildly funny.

Montreal is huge, much bigger than Vancouver. From the top of the mountain you can see skyscrapers and church steeples, lots of trees and grey stone buildings and little twisty streets running down from the mountain. You can see right across the St. Lawrence.

We made a quick stop at an outdoor market where they sold every fruit and vegetable I'd ever heard of and some new ones as well. I read the French signs and listened carefully to Luc and learned a few new words. I thought food words were the most practical ones to learn first.

Justine had lost interest in blue trucks. She was falling asleep in the car clutching her half-eaten apple. Luc was anxious to get her home, but he kept taking little detours to show me things along the way. I loved it. The streets looked like pictures of Paris.

"Naturally," Luc said. "Paris, Marseille, New Orleans, Montreal–the French are very good at cities."

Justine was beginning to whine and we decided it was time for her nap. When we arrived home Luc got out his cello and I listened to some scales and the beginning of a Bach suite. I recognized the music because Dad has the record. Finally, I decided to go off and have a look around the neighbourhood. All the houses were two or three storeys high and had outside staircases, either curved iron or straight wood, leading to balconies. When I got back Justine was awake and I helped her get dressed. She was cheerful again because we were going to pick her mother up at work.

Our conversation went like this. I would say, *"Camion bleu."* She would fall down on the bed giggling and I would grab a foot and put a sock on it. Then she would scream, *"Crème glacée,"* and I would say, *"Quoi?"* and she would shout even louder: *"Crème glacée."*

I took her across the park for ice cream.

The sun finally broke through as we left for Jeannine's craft store. She worked in a boutique where they had three floors of handmade crafts from all over the province.

Jeannine thought I should see the old section of the city. Luc objected. "But that's where the tourists go." She had the perfect answer. "Kate *is* a tourist."

And so I got to go for a ride through the oldest part of Montreal in a *calèche*, which is an old-fashioned horse-drawn carriage. The streets in this district are narrow and topped with cobblestones instead of pavement. The houses are all historical. We started out in Place Jacques Cartier and, sure enough, his actual house was still sitting there on the corner. Old Montreal was different from Louisbourg but I still had a feeling of people living in this place, going about their business, century after century. It's the sort of thing that history classes just never mention.

The bad thing about the *calèche* ride was Justine. She was scared of the horse. Jeannine held her on her knee and told her that there was nothing to be afraid of. We were all very nice to her, but little kids are not logical. She never once admitted that she was afraid of the horse. She just said she didn't like the way it smelled. She said it and said it and yelled it and screamed it until Luc asked the driver to stop. He and Justine got out and Jeannine and I continued our tour.

When we met them back at Jacques Cartier Square a few minutes later, Justine was happy again.

We all got together to make dinner. The phone rang just as I was putting the finishing touches to my dad's recipe for salad dressing. I heard Jeannine answer in French and then switch to English. She called: "It's for you, Kate." I picked up the phone. I hadn't felt a bit homesick until I heard Gram's voice.

I was back at the station the next morning, this time with Jeannine. We arrived six minutes before train time and struggled through the rush-hour crowd. We said *au revoir* in a hurry.

I got my own roomette right away this time. I moved in, putting my pictures on the wall and hiding my knapsack under the seat. As soon as the train pulled out of the station Fred dropped in to introduce himself. Fred is the best sleeping car conductor on the whole Via line and he has a very distinctive knock: one long, three short.

I decided to check out the snack bar. It was two cars down, walking backwards. That's what I call it when the train goes west and I go east, or vice versa. I stepped out of my compartment and bumped into Marjory, my neighbour right across the hall. She asked me to bring her back some tea from the snack bar.

I did and we had a great time all the way to Ottawa. The train stopped for two whole hours there. I didn't have anything to do, so Marjory suggested that I take a look at the Parliament Buildings. There was a special bus that went from the station to the centre of town and back again. Marjory was a travel agent and knew everything about visiting anywhere.

I made a friend in Ottawa. It wasn't the prime minister or a member of the House of Commons or even a Mountie, but he seemed to know his way around. I met him on the huge lawn outside the Parliament Buildings. I was a bit disappointed because they looked just like all the hundreds of pictures I'd seen. I don't know what I'd expected. I decided to take my own pictures anyway. Dozens of other tourists were doing the same thing.

I went way back on the lawn so that I could get everything in at once, but every time I was about to click the shutter I'd see a little white dog in the corner of my picture. It didn't seem right somehow. The Parliament Buildings are very serious. Finally I got a clear view. When I turned around, there he was, sitting right behind me wagging his tail. I checked the tag on his collar. His name was Spencer, and he'd had all his shots.

I guess he just decided I was the best person to spend the afternoon with because he followed me around until bus time. A Mountie trotted up on a big brown horse and everybody rushed over to take his picture too. I think that's the only reason he was there.

Spencer didn't like the horse and the horse didn't like Spencer and the Mountie was on the horse's side. He called down to me: "Is that your dog? He should be on a leash." For a minute I was afraid that Spencer might be arrested for annoying an official government horse on official government property, so I decided to pretend he was with me. "Sorry, officer," I said. "Come on, Spencer."

I looked up at the clock on the Peace Tower and decided there was time to take a walk along the canal. Spencer seemed to know exactly where we were going. We sat in the sun for a while and watched the cruise boat, and we played fetch the stick, which seemed to be his favourite game, until I started to worry about bus time and missing the train. I tried to leave him by the canal, but he trotted along after me all the way to the bus stop. I took a seat and looked out the window. The last I saw of Spencer, he was skipping down the main street on his way to the canal.

44

Back on the train, Marjory told me more about her job. She was travelling right across Canada, heading for Vancouver, like me. She was making up what she called a "package" for her travel agency–so that her customers would know all about hotels, restaurants and theatres and museums and beaches before they even left home. Naturally, Marjory had to try out all these things before she could recommend them. She'd started in Halifax and stopped in Fredericton and Montreal. She was going to skip Toronto because she lived there. Her next stop would be Winnipeg.

I asked her to tell me about Toronto since I was skipping it too. She said we'd see a bit of it from the train. The track ran right through downtown and we'd see a lot of skyscrapers. We'd even see the CN Tower. Marjory said the tower was the tallest building in the world but that sooner or later somebody somewhere would probably build something higher. Then she told me about the Science Centre where you can play with computers, and the special theatre just for kids, and the weird castle downtown and the islands right in the middle of the harbour where there are beaches and outdoor concerts.

When Marjory finally stopped talking about Toronto, I told her she could arrange a tour for me anytime.

46

W e made another stop in Kingston but I didn't get off this time. I just went for a walk through the train. I got to the Dayniter coach and that's where I ran into the strangest people I met on the whole trip. There were two of them: a man and a woman. They looked a bit alike, but it wasn't how they looked that made me sit near them, it was what they were doing.

They sat face to face. She brushed her teeth and then she combed her hair. He brushed his teeth and then he combed his hair. There was no comb and no toothbrush, but I knew exactly what they were doing. They were playing a mirror game and he was pretending to be her reflection. Every gesture he made was exactly the same as hers, only opposite.

Finally they sat back and smiled at me. Then the man reached down to the floor and pretended to lift something onto the seat between them. The woman smiled and nodded and began to unpack. I watched carefully: a bottle, two glasses and a corkscrew. She uncorked the imaginary bottle and filled the invisible glasses. They raised them in an exaggerated toast to me. I burst into applause and they bowed and sipped their wine. They still hadn't said a word.

I'd managed to stop laughing and was about to ask them who they were when the woman reached into the invisible box again and handed something across to me. What was it this time? I thought about it. A ham sandwich! I took a big bite, chewed and swallowed. Then I wiped my chin on a napkin and tossed it over my shoulder. That made them laugh.

He spoke first. "The kid's pretty good." She just winked and made the old okay sign with her thumb touching her first finger in a circle.

I stood up and bowed. She held out her hand. "Permit me to introduce us. I'm Susan and this is my brother William. We're known as the Silent Partners."

My two new friends were on their way to a festival in Toronto where mimes from all over the world were coming to perform and

48

talk to each other about not talking on stage. Susan and William could talk perfectly well, as it turned out, but I liked it best when they didn't, when all of a sudden one of them would freeze, then start to adjust a television set or play ping-pong.

Susan gave me a picture of the two of them in the costumes and white makeup they wore when they performed. William said that if I ever felt like running away from home, I could join their act. They needed an assistant to carry their props. "But you don't have any props," I told him. "You make them all up." "That's right," he said. "It's very light work."

I was having such a good time that I didn't even notice we'd arrived in Toronto until Susan reached for her suitcase and William pulled out an enormous handkerchief and pretended to cry. They backed off the train and onto the platform, weeping and waving and blowing kisses back to me. I hung out the door and watched them disappear into Union Station. Then I rushed back to tell Marjory all about them.

That night, I taped up my new picture on the wall beside the others and got right into bed. I could hear a train whistle wailing off in the distance and our own train answering. A long freight thundered past, with hundreds of boxcars heading the other way, back to Toronto. I looked up at the photograph of Susan and William in their costumes and funny makeup and wondered what they were doing just then. I was beginning to feel very sleepy...

...and the next time the whistle blew I was in a boxcar and we were pulling into Union Station, downtown Toronto.

I jumped down onto a wide, busy street and started to run, pushing my way through crowds of people on the sidewalk and darting between buses and cars at traffic lights. I turned a corner into an alley and climbed a fire escape to a door three storeys up. I knew it was a stage door and I knew it would be unlocked. I pushed it open and walked right in. Susan was pacing in the centre of the stage and William was leaning on an old wicker trunk. They were waiting for me.

Susan pointed to a full-length mirror at one end of the stage. I remembered that this was the land of mime where "no talking" was the rule. I looked at myself in the mirror, did a little dance and made some faces. I laughed–but not out loud.

William opened the trunk and handed me a violin. I tried it and made a terrible squawk. Susan shook her head. He pulled out a trombone. I blatted out a couple of notes and they covered their ears. I reached into the trunk for a French horn and tried again. Not a sound. Perfect.

Susan opened the door and we danced down the fire escape in single file. We were off to explore Toronto.

We ran uptown past stores and banks and restaurants and fountains. We skipped past streetcars and parking meters and Lake Ontario. We played invisible baseball and ate imaginary cheesecake. Then we were back in the alley, up on the iron staircase. We stopped in the middle for a concert. At the end of our performance, waves of applause rose up to greet us. Gradually the sound became louder.

It was the train, the wheels grinding on the rails.

I opened my eyes for just a second and smiled up at my partners on the wall. When I fell asleep again, they were running along behind the train, waving and acting crazy like they had that afternoon when we'd really said goodbye.

The next morning I met Marjory in the dining room for breakfast. She'd already finished, but said she'd be happy to have another coffee while I ate. Then we hurried to the observation car to look at Lake Superior. I liked the observation car. It had a big glass dome instead of a roof. At first, it was too misty to see much of the beautiful scenery that Marjory said was out there. After a while, the mist thinned out a bit and I saw that she was right. Every time we went around a bend or over a trestle bridge or headed for a tunnel, I'd jump up and take another picture.

Back in my roomette I couldn't get interested in my book or even writing in my journal. I looked out the window and wondered how we could possibly still be in Ontario. It seemed we'd been there forever, going past trees. My very rough estimate would be that the train passes at least fifteen billion trees on its way across Canada. Sometimes when you're by yourself you start to think about things that might seem dumb if you were busier. For instance, I don't know how long I must have spent sitting there thinking about trees. While I was doing it, I managed to make myself homesick for both homes at once. Newfoundland has tuckamore trees. They seem to grow right out of the rock and they twist and turn themselves into wonderful patterns. Gram always says that they're just like the people–sort of strong and brave and stubborn.

And spruce gum. Those trees made me think of Gram and her old gum that she used to peel right off the trunk to chew when she was a kid. Frankum she called it. She's actually admitted that she prefers sugarless spearmint these days, but that's all they could get back then.

One of my tricks, when I began to miss Woody Point, was to think about Vancouver and Dad. This time, because I was on the subject of trees, I remembered arbutus. Many people are of the opinion that the arbutus is the most beautiful tree in the world. My own father definitely thinks that. They have gnarled trunks–very different from the tuckamore, almost like a sculpture that you'd see in a park

somewhere. But the most spectacular thing about them is the colour of the bark, a dark orange. I once had the same shade in a set of paints and it was called burnt sienna.

So there I was sitting on the train just thinking about trees when Fred called in to see how I was doing. Fred never said he was the sleeping-car conductor. He always said he was in the sleeping-car business. He talked in short, fast sentences and it was usually hard to get a word in edgewise.

This time he said, "Well, how's the kid?" and before I could answer he went on: "Things are pretty slow in the sleeping-car business. Nobody sleeping. Nobody to wake up. No beds to make. Nothing doing. Thought I'd drop by. See what's keeping you so quiet.'

Now what is anyone supposed to say to that? I said, "Hi, Fred."

He passed me a soft drink. "Getting off at Winnipeg? Take a look around?"

I said that my next big stop would be a huge ranch in Saskatchewan where I would ride horses with my cousin Julie.

"Great town, Winnipeg. One of the best."

I wanted to talk more about how I would soon be galloping across the windswept prairie rounding up cattle and perhaps outwitting rustlers. So I said: "I guess I'll be seeing a lot of horses on our way through Manitoba."

"Not many in Winnipeg. They go in more for cats and dogs. Big city, Winnipeg."

"Bigger than Vancouver?"

"Well, Vancouver is crammed in there between the ocean and the mountains. Winnipeg can just spread out till the horses come home."

"Cows. Most people say till the cows come home."

That's the kind of crazy conversation I always had with Fred and it would always be cut off all of a sudden when his buzzer rang. Conversations with train conductors end abruptly on the buzz.

56

Marjory and I had a last dinner together in the dining car. We were both excited about our next stops. She had lots to do in Winnipeg and I was getting off at Regina the next afternoon. We traded addresses and promised to write each other. The best thing about travelling by train is the friends you make and we decided it's because there's nowhere to go and lots of time to talk.

I wanted to stay with Marjory until we reached Winnipeg. After all, it might be quite a while before I got to see her again. But she noticed me trying not to yawn and insisted that I go to bed. She said she'd sit up with me until I fell asleep or we arrived in Winnipeg, whichever happened first. She perched on the end of my bed the way Gram used to, and I talked to her about Newfoundland. For all Marjory's travels, she'd never been there. She'd never even been fishing.

Pretty soon the call came for Winnipeg and Fred arrived to help with her luggage. We hugged and kissed and reminded each other about visiting and then she was gone. I lay in bed looking out at the station, thinking that travelling is nothing but a series of hellos and goodbyes.

The next day the train felt almost empty. I spent the whole morning reading, and writing in my journal. Well, almost the whole morning. Fred kept popping in to make sure I was noticing the wheat fields and grain elevators outside the window.

When I went for lunch I saw an old woman at a table by herself. She looked up and smiled so I asked if I could sit with her. Her name was Helga Nielsen and she was eighty-three years old. I think that's the oldest person I've ever met. People always wanted to know what I was doing travelling alone, but when I told her about my trip she

wasn't at all surprised. She'd taken the train all by herself when she was even younger than me. In 1905 she'd travelled from Winnipeg to Pointe du Bois on a steam train called the Prairie Dog. She remembered her trip as though it had happened last year. She described the old wooden car with its squeaking wicker seats and the smell of the black smoke and cinders flying past the window. She said she could still see the conductor. When she told me his name had been Fred, I laughed so hard that I actually spilled my milk. I wondered if I'd remember this trip in seventy-five years. Maybe I'd be travelling to another planet, talking to a total stranger about Fred.

I went back to Mrs. Nielsen's seat with her. I thought I should help her with the between-coach doors, because she walked with a cane, but I don't think she really needed much help. I realized that she was old enough to be Gram's mother and that she was still doing the same things that she'd discovered were fun when she was my age.

Next stop: Julie's farm in Saskatchewan. Julie and I are distant relatives but we've never figured out exactly how distant. Dad says we're second cousins once removed, which may or may not be the same as third cousins. We were becoming less distant every minute now as the train raced to Regina. I opened my journal and started making a list that I called: Some Facts About Julie:

    very smart
    shorter than me (in spite of being two months older)
    loves horses (very good rider)
    wears glasses
    loves to stay up late and watch TV
    messy
    good handwriting (except when in hurry)
    has identical twin
    shy with new people.

There was one last thing that I didn't write. Although we were distantly related and even though she was probably my best friend, Julie and I had never actually met. A couple of years ago she scribbled a special message to me on their family Christmas card. I wrote back and since then we've been writing letters to each other. Even so, I was feeling nervous about actually meeting her.

When the call came for Regina, I lugged all my stuff down the passageway and waited by the door. The train stopped and Fred arrived to put down the stairs.

I was afraid I wouldn't recognize Julie, but of course there were two of her. I mean, there was Julie and there was Jill. I couldn't tell the difference but I figured that the person with them must be their oldest brother, Bob.

He came right up and said, "Hi, Kate," and took my bags from Fred. I stood there wondering which twin was Julie until they burst out laughing and put me out of my misery. "I'm Julie, she's Jill," said Julie. "Come on, let's go."

I turned around to say goodbye again to Fred, but he'd disappeared. We climbed into the back of a pickup truck and headed out of the city. Julie and Jill and I sat and stared at each other. We couldn't think of much to say. We sped along an absolutely straight highway past absolutely flat fields. I asked if they were wheat fields and Jill nodded. Every now and then we would slow down for a town. They looked just like the ones I had been seeing all day from the train: houses and stores half-hidden behind the huge wooden towers that I knew were grain elevators. I tried again to get a conversation going by asking what the towers were for.

"Wheat," laughed Julie. "It's all wheat. You know that, dummy." Somehow that insult was friendly. I laughed back at her and we began yelling over the noise of the truck about everything we'd been doing since our last letters.

At last we turned off the highway onto a gravel road. A family of deer dashed in front of the truck and we watched them leap away across the fields and out of sight. We pulled up between a grey stone barn and a bright yellow bungalow at the end of the road. Bob honked the horn and people came from every direction. It sure was a big family. Julie's mom came over and gave me a big hug. I felt funny for a minute because I didn't know what to call her. I knew her name was Maureen, but sometimes adults don't like kids to call them by their first names. Aunt Maureen was a bit strange because she wasn't really my aunt and I'd never met her before. Mrs. White sounded pretty stiff. I guess she read my mind because the first thing she said was: "I'm Maureen. You probably don't remember me because you were six months old the last time we met."

I got introduced to Julie's dad and two more sisters and two more brothers and then we filed inside for supper. I felt as if I'd stepped into a scene in one of those TV series where Mom and Dad sit at either end of the table and all the kids line up in between. That first meal was a bit strange for me–eating with so many people at once and having to

try several times before I got someone to listen to what I had to say. I'd never been in a big family before.

I shared a room with Julie and Jill. We talked for hours that first night and I guess we got pretty noisy because someone thumped on the wall from the room next door. We whispered after that.

Early next morning we headed for the barn. I had been picturing myself galloping over the prairie for so long, I couldn't believe it was going to happen. It wasn't as easy as I'd expected, though. Before you gallop over a prairie, you have to get on a horse, and Julie expected me to ride bareback. There wasn't even a stirrup to put my foot in or a saddle horn to hold on to.

Jill boosted me up while Julie held Star's bridle. I slid right over her back and ended up on the ground on the other side. The twins fell all over the barnyard laughing at me.

The second time I managed to stay put. Julie was on Flame, and Star followed Flame everywhere so I didn't have to worry about steering. We headed off at a slow trot. Julie kept glancing around to see if I was all right. Of course I was, so she kicked her pony and we were off. I hung onto the reins and hugged my knees into Star's ribs. We galloped all the way to the end of the gravel road before Julie reined in and turned around. Star stopped so fast I almost fell off. But I

felt wonderful. I could ride! I was on a real ranch and I was galloping across the prairie.

That afternoon everyone had things to do. Three sows were due to litter so that took care of Julie's dad and her oldest sister, Lorna. The three boys were working in the barn and Nancy, the other sister, was driving Julie and Jill into town for their swimming lesson. That left Maureen and me and the vegetable garden.

There were beans and carrots and beets and corn–everything that Gram had at Woody Point but about ten times more. There were also a lot of weeds and while we pulled and hoed, Maureen talked about my mother. I didn't really remember her at all but I knew about her, of course, from Dad and Gram. I'd seen lots of pictures and sometimes I thought I missed her, but it's not the same as missing somebody you know. She'd grown up on another farm, not far from here, and she was Maureen's cousin. I imagined her when she was my age, years before she met Dad. She must have spent every summer doing just what I did for those two days: weeding vegetables and feeding chickens and riding horses.

On my last night, we rode way up to the north pasture to herd the cows home for milking. I was a pretty good rider by this time. Star galloped and trotted when I wanted her to, not just when she made up her mind. The twins showed me how to round up cows. The trick was to get behind them and point them in the right direction. Once they get going, they don't stop. Cows don't have very much imagination.

I had a cow-milking lesson from Bob and then I wandered off and sat on the front porch by myself, looking at the sunset. The whole sky was streaked with pink and purple and orange. It seemed to stretch forever. The screen door slammed and Julie was beside me. We just stared at the sky for a while and then she said: "You'll be back on the train this time tomorrow."

I looked up at her. "I've had a great time here."

She nodded and reached for my hand. "Me too. Very nice to meet

you at last, Kate Reynolds." And we went in for supper.

The next day, I had the whole family pose in front of the house for an official portrait before Maureen and Julie drove me to Regina. We talked about Marcie. She was the oldest sister, the only one I hadn't met. She worked as a naturalist at the national park in Jasper and that was where I was heading.

Maureen was fine at the station–it was Julie who bugged me about not getting lost. I had to change trains in Saskatoon and she was convinced I would get confused and miss my connection.

The train between Regina and Saskatoon seemed like a toy compared to the huge Via trains I'd been on. It had one car with a built-in engine, like a bus on rails. The station at Saskatoon was big and bright and crowded. I knew I had to wait almost an hour for my next train. Everybody was with big groups of friends and nobody looked like they wanted to talk. I sat down by my suitcase and felt lonely.

There was an announcement that the train was going to be late. That made me more miserable. Finally they opened the gate and I marched straight through and up the platform to car one-forty-six, roomette nine. I didn't need any help finding it. I slammed the door and went right to bed.

When I woke up the train wasn't moving. I pulled up the blind and peered out into the early morning gloom. We were in the middle of a big city, probably waiting for the signal to go into the station. I propped myself up and thought for a minute. Edmonton. Then I fell asleep again, trying to remember whether it was the capital of Alberta or whether Calgary was.

We were coming into the Rockies that afternoon, so I went up to the observation car to get a good seat. I could see the mountains—they looked like low clouds on the horizon way off across the prairie. We stopped at a town that has the best name in Canada: Entrance. After Entrance you are really in the Rocky Mountains.

The station at Jasper was like a carnival with snack bars and souvenir stands and crowds of tourists with piles of luggage. It wasn't at all the way I thought a national park was supposed to be. I was struggling with my suitcase, wondering how I would ever find Marcie in all this, or how she would ever find me, when I noticed a tall woman coming straight toward me through the throngs of people pushing to get on the train. Up close, I could see that she looked a bit like her sister Lorna.

"So you're Kate!" she greeted me. She grabbed my bag and steered me through the station to her car. She had a thousand questions about Saskatchewan and her family and how things were going at the farm. I delivered all my messages. "Fine. They're all fine. They sent their love. Maureen will disown you if you don't visit in September."

We climbed into the car. Marcie was still talking. "There's far too much to show you in two days, but I'm going to do my best. We have a very tight schedule." Marcie didn't waste time. "We'll go see the glacier first and if we're lucky we'll catch some mountain goats on the way up." We crawled along the main street and she explained that from May to September it was rush hour all day long in Jasper.

We sped up once we got out of town. We twisted up a narrow mountain road and Marcie handled the hairpin turns without seeming to notice them. She told me all about her job as a naturalist for Jasper. She worked in special areas of the park, guiding tours, doing research on the plants and animals and giving lectures in the campsites.

We approached one last bend in the road and Marcie stopped talking. A huge wall of rock loomed ahead of us: Mount Edith Cavell. At first I just stared. I was trying to think of a word to describe how I felt.

Marcie laughed. "Overwhelming, isn't it?" I nodded. That was it. That was how I felt: overwhelmed.

We parked the car and hiked up the steep track for a closer look at the glacier. It was called the angel glacier because it looked like an enormous snow angel high up on the towering mountain side. It had pure white wings flecked with green where the snow was melting in the crevices. Marcie explained that it was receding now and that the valley we were walking through had been gouged out by the moving ice and snow hundreds of years before.

We circled the green lake at the foot of the mountain and climbed over· the ice until we were actually standing right on the glacier. Marcie said the crushed snow beneath us was deep enough to bury a highrise building.

On our way back down the mountain Marcie pulled off the road and pointed into the forest. A beautiful animal with huge, velvety antlers was peering back at us from the shadows.

"Elk," Marcie said. "It's very shy, so walk toward it slowly and quietly." I tiptoed across the road to take a picture. But some people in a big camper had noticed it too. They screeched to a halt in a cloud of dust and the elk vanished into the trees.

We stopped again when Marcie spotted a family of mountain goats grazing by the side of the highway. She handed me the camera.

"Are they timid too?" I asked.

"No, as a matter of fact they're quite social."

Back on the road, I got the naturalist's lecture on elk and mountain goats. Marcie knew that the elk we'd seen was a young one because he still had down on his antlers. We were lucky to have met him because elk avoid tourists as well as wolves and grizzlies. Mountain goats, on the other hand, are a very common sight in the park and everyone loves them. They have long, serious faces and they stare straight at you. Marcie said that later in the summer, when the kids become a little more independent, the herds travel up to the highest peaks in the Rockies. Their hoofs are like little suction cups and they can get around on glacial ice or rock that's almost vertical.

I put my last roll of film in the camera and explained to Marcie that I was saving it for a bear.

There are signs all over the park saying: "You are in Bear Country." All the campsites have bear-proof garbage cans and everywhere you go you find rules about how to behave when you meet a bear. The black bear is the symbol of Jasper National Park, and some of the naturalists there are studying the habits of grizzlies. All I can say about bears in Jasper is the whole time I was there I didn't see one.

We got up early the next morning and went straight to Marcie's office and she arranged for someone to take over her morning tour. She wanted to take me on the sky tram so that I could have a bird's-eye view of the park before I left.

The sky tram looks much scarier than it is. It's a little cable car that goes right to the top of the tallest mountain near the town of Jasper. What can you see from the peak? Well, you can see everything. The lakes look like bright blue puddles, and the town is just a bunch of toy houses off in the distance. Rivers twist through the mountain valleys like thin black-and-green ribbons. Marcie told me that the big river was the Athabasca and the others were tributaries. The highway and the railroad track are just barely visible. But mostly as far as you can see in any direction are the peaks of the Rocky Mountains covered in snow.

We scrambled into the car talking about train time. It had become a familiar conversation. It seemed I was on the verge of missing my train all across Canada, but I never once did.

There was one last treat. We stopped right in the middle of the highway outside the town to look at two deer. They were standing on the road ignoring all the cars and people. I thought they looked like bookends. I took a picture, of course—and it almost made up for not seeing any bears.

We got to the station in the nick of time. As we ran along the platform I told Marcie what a great time I'd had and how I loved her as much as all the rest of her family.

Suddenly a voice boomed, "All aboard! We can't wait even for you, Kate." I couldn't believe my ears. It was Fred.

We had a great evening together. I told him all about the ranch and horseback riding and Jasper and how mountain goats had suction-cup hoofs. While I'd been visiting, he'd been to Vancouver and back to Winnipeg and halfway back to Vancouver again. We opened the platform window and watched the sun set over Mount Robson, the highest peak in the Rocky Mountains–or at least in the Canadian Rockies. Fred just stood and stared, which is very unusual for Fred. When the sun disappeared behind the snow cap like a big red beach ball he snapped the window shut and said, "Time to get back into the sleeping-car business. See you in the morning."

I sat in the dining car for a long time after breakfast the next day. I was staring out the window, but not really seeing anything. It was all over. I did it. I crossed Canada. I looked after myself for fourteen whole days. In another hour I'd get off the train and Dad would be there to meet me.

Sooner or later he'd raise one eyebrow and say, "Well?" He had a special way of asking all about everything with that one word: "Well?" He'd really be asking about me and how I'd managed by myself and whether I'd been lonesome or forgotten to eat breakfast. He'd be asking about Gram and Woody Point and all our friends. He'd be asking about Canada.

Well?...Canada. I could say it's mountains and forests and skyscrapers and ghost soldiers from 200 years ago or prairie sunsets that almost make you cry and funny little kids running around counting *les camions bleus*. When I thought about it, I had lots to tell him.

I went back to my compartment to pack. Another half-hour to Vancouver, another half-hour to Dad.

But when I closed my eyes I was in Vancouver. I was back in the kitchen chopping carrots and Dad was laughing at me. I was out in the front yard with Yao, our dog that looks like a wolf, and we were singing *Oh, Susannah* together and Dad was yelling: "Keep it down! We have neighbours, you know."

We were in the park flying my almost-new kite that I got for my birthday a year ago and only used once. And we were down by the harbour at English Bay on our way downtown to visit Dad's office. And...

was the first one off the train. I saw him standing alone on the other side of the gate and I started to run. I stopped a couple of feet away and threw my suitcase down and just looked at him. He was smiling his wonderful Dad smile where his face crinkles up so that he looks like he's three years old and eighty both at once. I tackled him in the stomach and we had the world's longest hug. Then he stepped back and raised his left eyebrow and said, "Well?"

That night I got out my crumpled map of Canada and took him right across the country from Atlantic to Pacific. I introduced him to Fred and Marjory and brought him up to date on Luc and Richard and Maureen. I talked for hours. Finally I slowed down for a minute and he said, "Well!"

Then he picked up the phone and called Newfoundland. When Gram answered he said, "Mother, you were right."

I grabbed the receiver and started all over again at the Port aux Basques ferry. Gram just laughed at me.

"Stop! You're going to have to put it all down in the longest letter you've ever written."

The next morning I carefully wrapped up my journal and sent it off in the mail with the shortest letter I've ever written.

Dear Gram,

Here's "All Aboard!" for you to read.

love,
Kate

The authors gratefully acknowledge that...
Kate is
Kirstin Paterson
Gram is
Ella Manuel
Dad is
Brian De Beck

and in order of appearance...
Michel is
Peter Elgie
Richard is
John Fortier
Megan is
Meredith Willis
Charles is
Chris Willis
Luc is
Lesley Snider
Justine is
Marie-Justine Snider
Jeannine is
Jacinthe Snider
Marjory is
Myrtle Holloway
Susan is
Sharon Smith
William is
Whitney Smith
Helga Neilsen is
Minnie Muenscher
Julie is
Joyce Goudy
Jill is
Jenny Goudy
Bob is
Bruce Goudy
Maureen is
Marcie Goudy
Marcie is
Mirna Forester

Special thanks to:
Bill Coo, Alexa de Weil
and Spencer, Bill Goudy,
Brian Goudy, Douglas
Goudy, Laura Goudy,
Wanda Goudy, Sally
Paterson, Gaston Robèrge,
Karen Tallman De Beck,
John Webb, Nancy Willis,
Via Rail Canada Inc. and
staff, particularly "Fred"
and "Harold," Canadian
Kodak Ltd., The National
Museums of Canada, Parks
Canada, Tilden Rent-a-car
System Ltd., the Vintage
Locomotive Society
Winnipeg, Wintario, CN
Hotels, The Young
Naturalist Foundation, and
finally to Annabel Slaight
who made the adventure
possible.

Additional photo credits:
Toronto skyline:
    CN Tower
Goat: William K. Almond
Mount Robson:
    Miller Services

Designed by Nick Milton
Printed by
    Johanns Graphics Limited

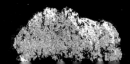

Canada: *Your own Trip*

You have just read about one young person's discovery of Canada. Of course, there are many thousands of other large and small trips one might take. Here are some ideas to get you, your family and friends thinking about a Canadian adventure of your own. Some addresses to write for further information are also provided.

Alberta

Population: 1,838,037
Capital city: Edmonton

Known as Canada's oil and gas province, Alberta also boasts a wealth of natural beauty. Its northern half is covered with great lakes, rivers and forests; rolling, treeless prairies stretch across the south, and overlooking it all are the magnificent snowcapped Rocky Mountains to the west.
But Alberta is much more than Canada's "wild west." Housed in Calgary's Glenbow Alberta Institute is the west's largest museum of human history and in Heritage Park you can ride a 19th-century stern-wheeler or an old steam locomotive.
At the wonderful outdoor museum at Fort Edmonton Park you can live a fur trader's life; and if you take the Dinosaur Trail from Drumheller you'll find yourself in a vast prehistoric graveyard, evidence that dinosaurs once roamed the area.

For more information write:
Travel Alberta, 10065 Jasper Ave., Edmonton, Alta. T5J 0H4 (403/427-4321).

British Columbia

Population: 2,466,608
Capital city: Victoria

Canada's most mountainous province, British Columbia is rich in natural resources. Salmon, cod and halibut abound off its deeply indented shore-line; fertile valleys have made the province famous for apples, peaches and other fruit; and, of course, in the Rockies there's a fortune in gold, silver and other minerals. Trees cover three-quarters of the province and these supply the country with much of its timber. For those who love the outdoors there is much to do and see here: there are massive glaciers at Glacier National Park, deep canyons and hot springs at Kootenay National Park, all sorts of wildflowers at Mount Revelstoke National Park and, if you are lucky, you can spot gray whales off Vancouver Island's west shore.
To see the province as it was in the past visit the 'Ksan Indian Village and Museum at Hazelton or the Barkerville Historic Park with its mining exhibits. Emily Carr's paintings at the Vancouver Art Gallery will also tell those who study them a great deal about British Columbia. And for a real treat see the world's tallest totem pole in Victoria. If only you could read the story it tells.

To find out what else British Columbia offers, write:
Tourism British Columbia, 1117 Wharf St., Victoria, B.C. V8W 2Z2 (604/387-6417).

Manitoba

Population: 1,021,506
Capital city: Winnipeg

Manitoba is not only a rich agricultural area, it's also one of Canada's most important commercial and sport fishing provinces. How so? Manitoba is dotted with thousands of sparkling lakes. Many people from many lands settled the province, and you can still see their influence today in such places as the reconstructed Mennonite village at Steinbach.
Another interesting journey back in time can be taken at Lower Fort Garry in Selkirk, the only trading fort in North America that's operating as it was in the mid 1800s.

Or in Winnipeg you can ride the Prairie Dog Central, a 1900s train operated by the Vintage Locomotive Society; visit the Manitoba Museum of Man and Nature; or see tumbleweed and other plantlife found only on the prairies at the Living Prairie Museum.

For more information write:
Manitoba Government Travel, 200 Vaughan St., Winnipeg, Man. R3C 1T5 (204/946-7131).

New Brunswick

Population: 677,250
Capital city: Fredericton

This province is an outdoors-lovers paradise with 14 million acres of forested land and 1,000 kilometres of seacoast. It's great fun to explore not only the cities and towns but the little fishing villages which dot the eastern and northern shores where English- and French-speaking fishermen have lived for many centuries. To discover all the fascinating stories of this province be sure to look in on Canada's oldest museum, the New Brunswick Museum, in Saint John. Or take a 90-

minute walk along the historic "Loyalist Trail" through the downtown—you'll even see a cage where, long ago, boys who misbehaved were locked away. Some surprises in New Brunswick include the Reversing Falls Rapids in Saint John where twice a day tides cause waters to flow upstream, Magnetic Hill near Moncton where your car will seem to coast uphill on its own, or the world's longest covered bridge at Hartland.

For more information write:
Tourism New Brunswick, P.O. Box 12345, Fredericton, N.B. E3B 5C3 (416/484-4867).

Newfoundland

Population: 557,725
Capital city: St. John's

This is Canada's newest province—it didn't join Confederation until 1949. It's a rugged, beautiful place with a 16,000-km coastline. Even in summer, if you're near Twillingate, you can see icebergs looming out of the water, and there are many places along the coastline to watch whales or seals. Newfoundland is a good place to imagine what it

was like to be a great explorer or pioneer, too. There are the remains of an A.D. 1000 Viking settlement to look at in L'Anse aux Meadows, at Cape Bonavista you can pretend you are John Cabot discovering America in 1497, or at Signal Hill National Historic Park in St. John's you can stand on a hilltop and be Guglielmo Marconi receiving the world's first transatlantic wireless radio message.
To learn more about the province's history visit the Newfoundland Museum in St. John's or the travelling *Norma and Gladys Schooner,* a sea-going museum.

For more information write:
Newfoundland and Labrador Tourism, Department of Tourism and Recreation, 130 Water St., St. John's Nfld. A1C 5T7 (709/737-2830).

The Northwest Territories

Population: 42,609
Capital city: Yellowknife

The Northwest Territories are so immense they cover one-third of Canada. The land is rocky and rugged,

interlaced by countless lakes and the mighty Mackenzie—one of the longest river in the world. Just over 500 km south of the Arctic Circle is Yellowknife, the largest settlement in the Territories and the place where gold was discovered in 1935. Today, you can still watch molten gold being poured into bricks at the Con Mine and see in the Museum of the North memorable photographs that capture the area's colourful history.
The white settler is a relative newcomer to the Territories. To dig deeper into the earlier history of the area, be sure to visit the Northern Life Museum at Fort Smith, where you can see early Indian and Eskimo tools, kayaks and even dinosaur bones. And if you want to visit the world's biggest buffalo herd in the world's largest national park, head for Wood Buffalo Natural Park at the Alberta/Northwest Territories border.

For more information on the Northwest Territories, write:
Travel Arctic, Yellowknife, Northwest Territories X1A 2L9 (403/873-7200).

Nova Scotia

Population: 828,571
Capital city: Halifax

Canada's earliest pioneers settled in this area in 1604, making this one of our most historically interesting provinces. At Port Royal National Park you can see what Canada's first permanent white settlement was like, or visit the old waterfront towns of Mahone Bay, Peggy's Cove, Lunenburg and Yarmouth, still looking much as they did two hundred years ago. Alexander Graham Bell had his summer home on Nova Scotia's Cape Breton Island and his Baddeck house is still filled with his inventions. Baddeck is also the start of a 100-km-long drive along the Cabot Trail through mountainous Cape Breton Highlands National Park.
To become part of 18th-century French life in Nova Scotia, visit the restored fort of Louisbourg; to become a miner, descend right into the coal pit underneath the Miners' Museum in Glace Bay; to become "salty tar," tramp about the decks of *Bluenose II,* a replica of the famous

racing schooner berthed in Halifax, or visit the oldest naval dockyards in North America and the naval museum there too.

For more information on Nova Scotia write:
Nova Scotia Department of Tourism, P.O. Box 130, Halifax, N.S. B3J 2M7 (902/424-5810).

Ontario

Population: 8,264,465
Capital city: Toronto

One of every three Canadians lives in this huge province and the lives its residents lead are varied indeed. In the rugged and mineral-rich northland, life is quite different from that in the well manicured and highly developed industrialized centres of the south. Canada's capital city Ottawa, straddling the border Ontario shares with Québec, is, of course, an important place to visit if you want to understand the country. Not only are there the Houses of Parliament to see but museums that can keep you busy for days. For a glimpse of our cultural and historical heritage there's the National Museum of Man, for inventions there's the Museum of Science and

Technology, for Canadian and European art there's the National Gallery of Canada—and this is only the beginning of the list. Toronto, Canada's largest city, has its share of interesting exhibits as well, with the Art Gallery of Ontario, the fascinating Royal Ontario Museum and the Ontario Science Centre competing for top honours. But, as cities and towns all over the province also have much to offer, a trip to Ontario has to be carefully planned.

For more information write:
Ontario Travel, Queen's Park, 900 Bay St., Toronto, Ont. M7A 2E5 (416/965-4008).

Prince Edward Island

Population: 118,229
Capital city: Charlottetown

Nicknamed "Spud Island" because of the 32 varieties of potatoes grown here, Prince Edward Island is Canada's smallest province and the only one completely surrounded by water.
Red earth, lobsters, oysters farmed in Malpeque Bay and the children's classic, *Anne of Green Gables*, written here by Lucy Maud Montgomery, have all made P.E.I. famous. But there's much more to see, including the room in Charlottetown where the Fathers of Confederation planned the formation of the country in 1864. Two other interesting places are The Acadian Museum and Pioneer village at Miscouche and the Micmac Indian Village at Rocky Point.

For more information write:
Tourism Services, PE.I. Department of Tourism, Parks and Conservation, P.O. Box 2000, Charlottetown, P.E.I. C1A 7N8 (902/892-2457).

Quebec

Population: 6,234,445
Capital city: Quebec City

Canada's largest province is home to most of this country's French-speaking population. (In fact, Montreal is the second largest French-speaking city in the world.) The province is unique for its combination of natural beauty and its sense of culture and history. It contains many beautiful wilderness parks, such as the Formillon National Park in Gaspe; North America's only walled city—Quebec City—where you can step right into history just by walking its cobblestone streets. Or you can visit such well-preserved historic sites as Plains of Abraham in Quebec City where Generals Wolfe and Montcalm fought their famous 1759 battle. You can learn even more about early French Canadian life in the city's Musée du Québec. Montreal, too, has its share of places to catch up on Canada's past, especially in the Vieux Montréal area.

For more information write:
Quebec Ministry of Tourism, Hunting & Fishing, 150 Boul. Saint Cyrille E., Quebec City, Que. G1R 4Y1 (418/643-2280).

Saskatchewan

Population: 921,323
Capital city: Regina

The first white man to see the vast buffalo herds that once roamed the Saskatchewan plain probably did so about 1690. But settlement in this beautiful province with the big, dramatic sky and endless billowing grasses didn't really begin here until the mid-19th century. You can get some ideas how early pioneers lived at the 1864 Hudson Bay outpost of Fort Qu'Appelle, or in the 19th-century town that has been recreated at Moose Jaw. Because of all the bones left there by generations of buffalo hunters, Saskatchewan's capital was once called Pile of Bones. Its name was changed to Regina in 1882 to honour Queen Victoria and there is much to see here, including the Indian relics at the Saskatchewan Museum of Natural History, the restored home of former Prime Minister John Diefenbaker and the camp where all Mounties get their training.

For more information write:
Extension Services, Saskatchewan Tourism and Renewable Resources, 1825 Lorne St., Regina, Sask. S4P 3V7 (306/565-2300).

The Yukon

Population: 21,836
Capital city: Whitehorse

One of Canada's last frontiers, the Yukon is the land of the midnight sun filled with memories of gold rush days. The museum at Dawson City—once a bustling boom town with a population of 30,000—recalls the 1896 heyday when gold was first discovered. But the Yukon is more than gold rushes and ghost towns: it's the site of spectacular ice fields, Canada's highest mountains, great rushing rivers and vast tracts of unspoiled wilderness with an abundance of wildlife, including the ruggedly beautiful Kluane National Park.

For more information write:
Yukon Department of Tourism, P.O. Box 2703, Whitehorse, Yukon (403/667-5340).

P.S. Be on the lookout for the *Discovery Train*, a special project of the National Museums of Canada. This travelling museum on wheels is touring across Canada and may stop at a city near you!

Canadian Cataloguing in Publication Data

Allinson, Beverley, 1936-
    All aboard

ISBN-0-919872-43-3 bd. ISBN 0-919872-44-1 pa.

I.O'Kelly, Barbara, 1945-   II.Title.

PS8551.L556A74   jC813'.5'4   C79-094429-4
PZ7.A45All